THE ART OF CONVERSATION

HOW TO COMMUNICATE EFFECTIVELY BY REFINING YOUR SOCIAL SKILLS

STEPHEN HAUNTS

STEPHEN HAUNTS LTD

Paperback ISBN : 9781710541441

CONTENTS

This book is dedicated to my wife Amanda and my kids, Amy and Daniel.

ALSO AVAILABLE FROM STEPHEN HAUNTS

https://geni.us/thepathtofreedom

ABOUT THE AUTHOR

Stephen Haunts has been a professional software and application developer since 1996. Stephen has worked across many industries, including computer games, online banking, retail finance, healthcare and pharmaceuticals and insurance.

Stephen is also an experienced development leader and has led, mentored and coached teams in the delivery of many high-value, high-impact solutions. Outside of his day job, Stephen is also an experienced tech blogger who runs a popular blog called *Coding in the Trenches* at www.stephenhaunts.com, and he is also a training-course author for the popular online training company Pluralsight.

WHY I WROTE THIS BOOK

At the start of my career — over twenty-five years ago — I struggled with talking to people. I was very introverted and shy. I would actively avoid trying to speak to people in-person and on the phone. One of the reasons I enjoyed software development so much in my early career was because it was a relatively solitary career. That was until the scope of the projects I was working on grew larger, along with the teams I worked with. In my early career, I found teamwork difficult, but I had to adapt and overcome my anxiety about speaking to people. It wasn't so bad with my teammates because I got to know them over many years, but it was hard meeting corporate clients and business sponsors.

I knew I had to do something about being shy and struggling to talk to people that I was not comfortable with. Getting over social anxiety and becoming good at talking to people isn't something that can be accomplished overnight. It took me many years to become comfortable. I am still an introvert. That will never change, but I don't consider myself shy anymore. Not all introverts are shy, but some are. Believe it or not, there are also shy extroverts. Just because they recharge their mental batteries in the company of others doesn't mean they are automatically good at conversation.

Later in my career, I started recording training courses for a US company called Pluralsight. Pluralsight is an online training platform that is a little like Netflix, but instead of films, you watch training courses on various subjects. To make these courses a success, I had to promote them. Part of this was done through social media and blogging, but I also wanted to start public speaking because that would put me in direct contact with my target audience at conferences. Getting the courage to speak on stage took a lot of effort, practice and mental readjustment, but I eventually achieved it. I would now say that I truly enjoy being on stage talking to people.

This book isn't trying to turn you into a public speaker. I don't want to scare you off, but this book will help you try to break away from your fear of speaking to people.

In this short book, I want to give you a simple

roadmap you can follow to improve your conversational skills. The book isn't a silver bullet for conversation success. No one could ever claim to have that, but if you put into practice the techniques I discuss and work at trying to become a great conversationalist, then you can become more comfortable.

I have attempted to keep this book short. The reason for this is that, if you are suffering from social anxiety, then you probably don't want to wade through a 300-page textbook. This book can comfortably be read through in one or two sittings. I recommend reading the book through in its entirety and then working out how you can start applying each step and putting it into practice.

Good luck and all the best.

UNDERSTANDING YOUR PERSONALITY

R elating to others can seem like an insurmountable task for some people. Walking up to a co-worker, friend or stranger to start a conversation may seem like a nightmare come to life, but it doesn't have to be like this. Even if someone feels they are the only person in the room too nervous to interact with others, it is important to remember that they are likely not alone. Breaking the conversational ice starts from within. Once a person takes a deeper look at themselves and their own needs, speaking up can become much easier.

In this chapter, will discuss how a person can assess and understand their personality to better create social interactions that will allow them to work within their limitations. We will go over the benefits of leaving your comfort zone and how to approach the challenges that come with such a decision.

Understanding and Assessing Personality Types

Before someone can begin relating to others in a social context, it can be helpful for that person to do a little preparatory research about themselves. There are many online tests claiming to be the leader in distinguishing between personality or temperament types. The determination of personalities, however, began with Hippocrates in roughly 450 BC.

Hippocrates created the idea that personality traits and human behaviours are based on four separate temperaments associated with the four fluids (humors) of the body. These personality types are — choleric, phlegmatic, sanguine and melancholic. All of these categories focus on a person's attention span and persistence in the task at hand. Choleric people are typically easily distracted yet persistent in everything that they attempt. Those who are sanguine are also easily distracted and lack dedicated persistence in completing complex tasks. The phlegmatic and melancholic temperaments are both very focused, with phlegmatic trumping its competitor in that it tends to be the more tenacious of the two.

Later, other philosophers would adopt Hippocrates's theory but focus on medical factors instead of the four humors of the body. These ideas developed over time and eventually led to the personality tests that you see in use today.

When discovering your personality type, you need to remember that there are different versions of yourself to take into account. Your personality can change depending on the specific environment you are in, such as home or work. Also, your personality will change over time, as you get older and more experienced. With this being said, you are likely to have a set of core personality traits that have been with you throughout your life, from childhood to adulthood.

One test now stands out in the crowd of assessments — the Myers-Briggs personality test. This detailed appraisal of someone's preferences uses the test taker's responses to plot how they are most likely to interpret or react to situations in the real world. It includes 16 personality types composed of combinations of four letters. It considers how someone prefers to spend their time, how they handle different situations, and how they process information and their decision-making process. These responses are recorded to categorise a person as either introverted or extroverted, judging or perceptive, sensing or intuitive, and thinking or feeling. Each unique combination makes up a different personality. Taking the Myers-Briggs test can give further insight into someone's key personality areas.

The Myers-Briggs test is a test that you have to pay for, but there are similar alternatives available on-line that you can take for free. My personal favourite is a website called 16 Personalities (www.16personalities.com). You can see my latest results in the following screenshot.

My personality type was classed as an Architect (INTJ-T). The description taken from the 16 Personalities sites classifies an architect as follows:

It can be lonely at the top. As one of the rarest personality types – and one of the most capable – Architects (INTJs) know this all too well. Rational and quick-witted, Architects may struggle to find people who can keep up with their nonstop analysis of everything around them.

From my results, I am very introverted. I like my own space and recharge my mental batteries by being on my own. I like to use my intuition and I tend to overthink problems and situations. According to the 16 Personalities website, my traits are also shared by the following famous people: Friedrich Nietzsche, Michelle Obama, Elon Musk, Christopher Nolan, and Arnold Schwarzenegger.

Assessing your own personality type can help you learn where you can push yourself and what your limits are. For example, introverts tend to thrive on quiet, alone time — something I can relate too. They often need time to process the day and think through upcoming tasks. Knowing this, an introvert can limit their social exposure so that they are never overloaded when interacting with others. Introverts can schedule times in the day to sit in quiet reflection and gather their thoughts before going back into the world. Extroverts, however, thrive on interacting with others. If they were stuck in the house alone all day, it would likely be a horrible day for them. Even extroverts who are timid and not prone to long conversations with strangers can meet their social needs by going to public places. Sitting in a coffee shop or walking around a shopping mall can simulate the interactive experience and quell the extrovert's need for other people.

In the same vein, it can be helpful for a person to know if they prefer detailed planning or spontaneous events. For someone who enjoys planning out their day, it can be easy to schedule time to be social and practice their conversation skills. Having such a schedule written down also gives the person a chance to mentally prepare for the situation. Leading a meeting or volunteering in a collaborative project at work are both ways you could schedule social interaction with other people. Someone who prefers spontaneity may, instead, rely on water-cooler conversations or witty banter with the cashier at the grocery store or a stranger at the train station. These impromptu interactions can help ease your general anxiety about speaking to others via consistent practice in unplanned conversations. Assessing your personality traits and pairing them with your social needs creates a blueprint for approaching daily interactions and conversations with other people.

Staying in Your Comfort Zone

People create their own comfort zones with activities that make them happy, such as watching TV, reading, or scouring the Internet and social media. By surrounding themselves with these comforting activities, such people do not have to experience pain and can remain in control of their environment. These sorts of actions are a type of emotional barricade to keep out unwanted feelings. You can become aware of your comfort zone by imagining something that might cause pain and then examining how you could structure your life around this pain. For example, if someone hates going to restaurants, they may see to it that they only order food via delivery or cook in their home. They may even avoid having dinner with family or friends if these individuals have chosen a restaurant instead of someone's home. Such a person would be going out of their way to remain safely in their comfort zone.

Staying in a comfort zone can lead to missing out on life experiences you may enjoy. Someone who is afraid to travel may never leave their hometown if they choose not to push the boundaries of their safe space. This means they never see the world beyond the area where they grew up, which can amount to missed experiences and lessons not learned.

To leave their comfort zones, people have to be willing to embrace the pain that comes with stepping outside of them. Many experiences beyond a comfort zone will register as immediate panic or discomfort, but often, if someone sticks with such an activity, they are able to realise that it is not as painful as they anticipated. Learning to embrace the pain means that the person accepts that attempting something outside of their comfort zone may be difficult but also realises that the experience is worth the challenge. Embracing the pain of the unknown leads to increased confidence and a sense of power. Once a person realises they are able to overcome their fears, they can continue to do so throughout their life.

Once someone has embraced the pain and left their comfort zone, they can experience the rich adventures this world has to offer. Overcoming fears gives a person the ability to confidently go into the world and tackle any challenge life throws at them. They are also able to experience the world without the constant fear that something might go wrong. The more confident someone becomes, the more they realise that their fears are not as imposing as they initially seemed, which can drive them to overcome more of their fears. It is a productive cycle of self-affirming success.

Embracing Positive Change

Anxiety is widespread and affects everyone differently. In fact, anxiety affects about 40 million people older than 18 in the US and is one of the most prevalent mental illnesses.

Social anxiety is the fear of being in social settings and interacting with others, often stemming from the fear of being judged. People's social anxiety can range from mild to crippling, depending on their anxiety levels and past experiences. It can be difficult for people with social anxiety to engage in conversations or attend social outings without feeling uncomfortable. This discomfort stems from an "inner critic" who is constantly telling the person things like they are being judged or are not good enough. This critic is, of course, the person's own mind preying on their fear.

Challenging such negative thoughts is imperative in overcoming social anxiety and fostering confidence. If negative thoughts are allowed to rule a person's decisions, then it can be incredibly difficult to overcome social anxiety. Making a concerted effort to ignore intrusive thoughts can help someone overcome their anxiety and possibly even enjoy social situations.

One way to challenge these intrusive thoughts is to imagine the absolute worst-case scenario and then assess how likely it is the imagined situation will occur. For example, if a person is afraid of public speaking, they might imagine a scenario in which they mess up a line and the audience laughs them off the stage. After taking a step back and considering the scenario rationally, however, the person could remind themselves that people are generally understanding and they might have even seen multiple professional speakers misspeak and continue to give a successful speech. This can calm anxious nerves and help to convince the person that everything will be okay, even if the worst-case scenario happens.

A person can replace self-deprecating thoughts with an argument for why the trait in question is desirable. For example, if someone has it in their mind that their sense of humour is not widely appreciated, they could argue that more people wished they had a niche sense of humour instead of the blanket jokes everyone has heard before. Turning a negative into a positive helps create an appreciation for the traits the person possesses.

Another tactic with which to silence critical thoughts is to embrace them with self-affirming put-downs to acknowledge the source of nervousness while, at the same time, building confidence. If someone is nervous about being clumsy, they could say something like, "Oh yeah, I could win an Olympic gold medal for clumsiness." This makes light of the trait while affirming to yourself that it is something to be proud of.

Overcoming social anxiety starts with accepting a challenge. This might be to say hello to a stranger or participate in small talk by the water-cooler at work; whatever the task, it can be difficult for someone with anxiety. There are a number of tricks to overcome the initial fear that comes with starting a conversation with a stranger, but to solve the root of the problem, it is suggested people expose themselves to the root of the fear in small doses. This approach is called exposure therapy.

Exposure therapy can help someone confront a frightening situation and gradually become more comfortable with it. The process is simple — a person will identify something that causes anxiety or fear in them and begin exposing themselves to that thing in small doses. For example, if someone is afraid of snakes, they might go to the zoo and look at the snake exhibit every day until they begin to feel more comfortable. The exercise should only be performed for as long as it takes the person to feel comfortable with the situation. The goal is to take less time getting comfortable at each exposure and build up a sort of tolerance to the situation. Over time, the person should be able to tolerate more and more time in the uncomfortable situation without intense levels of fear or anxiety. Eventually, the fear may disappear completely.

Although this may sound like a fairly simple way to address social anxiety, a person should understand the emotional toll of the process before beginning it. In the initial exposure, a person can expect to feel a shock of anxiety or intense fear, which may make them want to discontinue the practice. However, it is important to persevere through the initial negative feelings so that a person can teach themselves that the situation is not harmful and does not need to evoke a negative reaction. Someone pursuing exposure therapy should keep in mind that the process takes a long time and considerable dedication if it is to work properly.

To ease the transition into social interaction, people often join like-minded groups or organisations so that there is a common and relatable topic of conversation. Being in groups of people with similar interests can help to ease anxiety because this can feel similar to the safe space a person would create for themselves. Knowing everyone in the group has a common interest immediately generates conversational topics and a common motive to bond over.

A person decides who will surround them in life, and it is important to choose supportive friends who celebrate one another's quirks and differences. For those with social anxiety, having a support system of people who understand anxiety can be a tremendous confidence boost. Groups can help people practice speaking to strangers or new people in a safe space, in which they will not be judged or forced to act before they are ready.

Surrounding yourself with people who have similar interests and goals makes approaching people easier; the common ground is a conversation-starter that has the potential to lead elsewhere or merely give someone practice in interacting with different types of people. Interacting with people in a group can also lead to meeting new friends through networking. Groups are a great place to be introduced to new people and grow a personal social network. The more friends a person has, the greater chance they will find someone they are comfortable sharing their opinions with.

2

THE POWER OF CONVERSATION

S peaking to others, even familiar people, can be terrifying for those with social anxiety. The bene- fits of conversation, however, far outweigh the costs. People are hard-wired to crave interaction, and they derive important reactions from conversations. This hard wiring is sometimes still not enough to push people into action, though. When someone finds social interaction too scary, they may isolate themselves and become lonely. Loneliness has many negative effects, both physical and emotional. Speaking with others staves off loneliness and can help ease anxiety and stress over time. Sometimes, the best way to start talking to others is to join a group of like-minded people and embrace the fear of becoming a part of something larger. It can be intimidating to enter a group of people who know each other already, to be the new kid on the block, but eventually, such a situation can become a safe space away from home in which to express ideas and opinions with people who share the same values. The key to blending in with established group members is to know the rules and respect the goals of the group.

This chapter discusses the harmful effects of remaining isolated and the benefits of interacting with others. This chapter will offer tips on how to overcome the fear of speaking with others and set social goals to ensure regular social interaction with others. We will also discuss the benefits of joining groups and how to become the ideal group member.

Feelings

Humans are innately social creatures, who typically value social interaction more than almost anything else. We evolved living in groups, and our psychology still desires group interaction and collaboration to meet our social needs. Even people with social anxiety, who may struggle with interacting with others, need the benefits conversations can give them.

Without consistent interaction with others, people can become increasingly lonely. Whether it is brief or prolonged, loneliness is a pervasive issue in society. Those who are not comfortable speaking around others may isolate themselves, depriving their brain of the happy feelings that come from speaking to others. Feeling as if they are not part of a community can lead to negative effects on both mental and physical health.

Loneliness can cause physical effects such as high blood pressure and weight gain. It can potentially lead people to pick up other bad habits, such as smoking, which may help ease their anxiety, and cause them to reduce their exercise. People who are lonely usually lose interest in their normal daily activities and may prefer to stay inside, in their comfort zones, instead of pushing their boundaries to benefit their mental health.

These psychological symptoms of loneliness can do more than just alter your behaviour; they can raise stress hormones, which negatively impacts the immune and cardiovascular systems. When someone has anxiety or is depressed, it is not uncommon for their stress hormones (cortisol) to increase because their body can perceive what should be a normal situation as a threat. This increase in stress forces the immune system to work over-time to compensate for the inflammation caused by stress hormones. The heart also has to work harder because stress often correlates with an increased heart rate, which is a part of fight-or-flight response.

Being lonely can cause a person to be hyper-sensitive to social cues, which compounds the fear their anxiety induces and can cause them to continue avoiding the interaction they need. An anxious or lonely brain is usually looking for reasons to stop its exposure to scary situations. This means that someone who is having a conversation despite their anxiety may be more attuned to the nonverbal cues of their conversational partner, but they may not necessarily interpret them correctly. The anxious person will often see such cues as negative feed-back based on their words and actions, signs the other person does not enjoy interacting with them. In the event they do have a successful conversation, they often attribute success to dumb luck and not their hard work. This makes it difficult for these people to recognise that their hard work and bravery are paying off, which means they may not try to face their fears again.

In addition to struggling to correctly interpret social cues, it can be more difficult for a lonely person to fight through day-to-day disruptions and work out common problems. This is because they have an inherently nega-tive view of themselves and, instead of working through a problem or ignoring a disruption, they may be inclined to think that the cause of it is themselves. This can lead to negative self-talk and create a vicious cycle of low self-esteem.

Working to increase social exposure, despite anxiety, can help combat the negative effects of loneliness and make someone feel more engaged and accepted. Although it may feel scary or seem difficult, breaking out of the bubble and embracing social interaction is the best thing for a lonely person. It meets the need for community, which reinforces positive thoughts and feelings.

When a person does intend to interact with others, it is important for them to remember that empathy is one of the most effective ways to relate to others. Empathy is the practice of imagining yourself in another person's position, that is, thinking about how a situation would make the other person feel, and responding based on that inference, instead of merely the information someone is conveying.

Empathy promotes social behaviour by creating the desire to help other people and act compassionately. People are typically drawn to emotional connections, so when someone reacts empathetically, it makes them feel like someone cares. This reaction often makes a person feel more comfortable speaking openly and sharing their thoughts. Another way to demonstrate empathy is through body language. People can read social cues such as facial expressions and posture and tend to mimic these as an expression of empathy to the other person. Mimicking body language shows the speaker that the listener is on the same page and cares about the outcome of the conversation.

Researchers distinguish between two types of empathy: affective and cognitive. Affective empathy deals with the emotions we feel in relation to someone else's feelings, and cognitive empathy refers to mentally putting yourself in the place of someone else. In other words, affective empathy is the way other people's feelings make us feel, and cognitive empathy is imagining how the other person feels.

The human inclination toward empathy is rooted in evolutionary psychology. In the caveman days, empathy might be the deciding factor between life and death. If a person was unable to pick up on someone else's fear, they might not realise they were in a dangerous situation. Empathy also helps form connections, which can keep groups together, and living in groups was critical to survival in early human history.

Empathy can help to reverse the harmful symptoms of anxiety and loneliness because it can lower stress hormone levels. When a person is empathetic, they have a better ability to regulate their own emotions, which means less stress over feelings they cannot control. With lower levels of stress hormones in the body, the immune and cardiovascular systems can take a break and return to normal function. This regulation of the emotions can even help people fight feeling burned out at work because empathy teaches the body to react to difficult situations in a healthy, metered way. Knowing that not every stressful situation needs to be met with an overtly emotional response can help people regulate their work stress. When someone is able to do this, work may not seem so terrible and stressful anymore.

Taking Action

Once someone is comfortable with confronting their social anxiety, they should consider taking action to increase their exposure to social situations. It can be scary to make the first move in a social interaction, but it is key to overcoming social anxiety. There are a variety of opportunities to start conversations as well. A person could talk to co-workers, sign up for a class or join a volunteer group to find people to speak to.

The more a person exposes themselves to different groups, the more opportunities they create for new friendships to interact with others. These opportunities are invaluable for creating a social network that a person can rely on. Having a dependable group of people to interact with can spare someone from becoming lonely and serve as a practice arena for conversation.

Some people with social anxiety may realise that joining a group could be beneficial for them and even make plans to attend but never quite have the courage to follow through on these plans. To ensure these activities are not only theoretical, a person should make concrete efforts to join when they are feeling particularly coura-geous. A moment of empowerment can be a great time to sign up for something scary if you promise yourself you will not back out afterwards. Signing up for something non-refundable is a great way to ensure attendance, even if the person is nervous.

Setting goals can help foster a determination to follow through with social commitments, but they must be created in a specific way so as to ensure follow-through. The goal should always be specific and attainable. Some people set goals too high too fast, and it can be discouraging when they are unable to reach them right away. Creating a set of steps to achieve a specific goal is a tactic that can prevent people from becoming discouraged when they realise that reaching their dream will take longer than anticipated. As a person takes each of the steps toward their goal, they can celebrate these small victories and stay encouraged to keep working to the end.

Another helpful way to prepare for achieving a goal is to list potential obstacles before starting. If a person can sit down and identify all the things that might go wrong or deter them from reaching their goal, they can plan for how they will overcome these obstacles if they arise. Part of this planning is about setting deadlines for goals, both large and small, to keep a person on track. With a set date, people are encouraged to work to meet their goals in a realistic timeline, instead of languishing in unaccomplished steps. If a person is having trouble meeting their deadlines, they can schedule dedicated time to make progress toward their goal so that they know they are working on it every day and making progress.

If someone's goal is to join a group, they can remember that becoming ingrained in a group of like-minded people can create a safe space within that social situation. Although the first meeting may be awkward and scary, as someone gets to know the group they've joined, they can become more comfortable around the other group members. That way, if the group hosts others, the person can still feel safe among strangers because there are people around who they know and who know them.

To be part of a group, a person should understand the purpose of the group and keep that at the forefront of their mind when interacting with its members. For example, if someone joined a charity, they should remember to always be kind and giving as a way to exemplify the values of that organisation. It is important for a person to join a group they truly identify with and not just one intended to force social interaction. If someone with anxiety joined a group they had no interest in, it could make conversation more stressful and difficult, therefore creating a negative experience.

Groups are all about cohesion, and a good group member will understand the rules of the group and abide by them. Some groups are more personal than others, such as small book clubs or dinner clubs, as compared to a local mental health awareness or homeless shelter volunteer group. In the first two settings, it is more likely that the members would share personal details with one another and deviate from the topic at hand. The last two settings, however, may be more focused on the task at hand and completing a project than small talk. Respecting the conversational boundaries in a group is imperative in becoming an accepted member.

It is worth noting that joining a group does not ensure a relationship with every member. Someone breaking into a new group should expect to get to know the members slowly, one or two at a time, until the other members make an effort to get to know them one-on-one. Especially in large groups, there may be some people in the group that the person will never be close with, but as long as they have connected with other members, it is okay.

Unfortunately, not all groups are a good fit for everyone. If a person finds themselves in a group they do not feel connected to, they may need to consider finding a new one that more closely aligns with their values. Just as not all friendships work out, not all groups will work out either. There may be no one there a person feels they can connect with, or the focus of the group may not be as interesting as anticipated. No matter the reason, it is okay to leave a group if it is not helping to meet your social needs.

If the group is a match, though, its conversations can become a breeding ground for ideas, all stemming from different people, making it easy to get lost in the noise. Especially in the first group conversation a person attends, it can be helpful to remain mostly quiet. This will allow such a person to feel safe and slowly process the flow of conversation. Group conversations lend themselves to cross-talk, and it may be difficult to know where to jump in, so staying quiet until you figure out which conversation to join is a safe tactic. Not everyone in a group needs to command the stage, and often, being a great listener is valued just as highly as someone who is very communicative. Once a person comes to understand how the group members speak to one another and finds a topic they can contribute to, they should jump in with their opinion to show they want to participate.

For a person to ensure they are not sitting silently for the entire group discussion, they can set a time limit on how long they are allowed to be quiet before chiming in. This helps to make sure a person isn't using the noise level or complexity of a conversation as an excuse not to participate. Someone can pick a timeframe, such as 10 minutes, and decide that no more than that amount of time can pass without them speaking. This tactic can work especially well in established groups, where it may be difficult to find a logical place to jump in.

Chiming in doesn't mean someone has to offer insightful opinions or introduce new topics, though. A person can simply interject a "yeah" or "no kidding" and still be seen as participating in the conversation. This simplifies contributions and is often less nerve-wracking than airing one's own ideas or opinions. It shows a person is involved in the conversation and willing to engage but doesn't require an exhausting amount of effort on the part of the person with social anxiety.

Not all conversations are easy to jump into, however. Some group discussions can get loud and disorganised, which makes it difficult to track who is speaking and even what the topic is. In these situations, it is important for a person to accept that their comments may not have the attention of the entire group. Side conversations may be the most attention they'll receive, and that can sometimes be a good thing. Instead of focusing on the bothersome parts of these types of conversations — volume, side conversations and interruptions — a person should focus on creating a small environment that can sustain the information they have to share. This way, they are able to gain practice interacting with others without disrupting the flow of the group.

Sometimes, a person will end up in a conversation about a topic they know nothing about, but using this as an opportunity to relax can help ease the tension once the subject changes again. When the subject moves to something unfamiliar, an anxious person can take the time to sit back and catch their breath after contributing on previous topics. Enjoying the time to recoup social energy and think about their next contributions can be rejuvenating for socially anxious people. Once the topic has fizzled out and the conversation has moved on, they can feel free to jump back in with their renewed energy.

Groups appreciate responsive listeners; this is a way to interact with members nonverbally if the topic is not something a person feels comfortable contributing to. Nodding when people make legitimate points and making eye contact with the speaker shows attentiveness and interest. Without speaking, the listener can show their interest and refrain from disrupting the conversation.

If a person is put on the spot about being too quiet in a group, the best way to handle the situation is for them to own their disposition. There is nothing wrong with being quiet in conversation, and there is nothing wrong with letting people know this. Two ways to approach explaining this idea to people are turning it into a joke, such as saying, "I'm speaking telepathically with Beth," and admitting to it and letting people react how they will.

3

THE IMPORTANCE OF LISTENING

Once someone has grasped starting to speak or interact in a conversation, it's time to think about being on the other end of a social interaction — listening. Listening is an important skill, and it helps reciprocate the exchange of ideas in conversations. It can be more complex than it sounds, though, and effective listening requires consistent effort. Every person wants to be heard. It fulfils innate human needs. Active listening is one of the best ways to demonstrate interest and concern while someone is speaking. This can work in both group and one-on-one situations. When mastering how to perform effective listening, it is important to know the difference between listening and hearing. Listening requires more focus and goes deeper than simply hearing someone speak.

Another important aspect of conversations is silence. Silence can signal a number of different things in a conversation, and if someone is listening, they will be able to easily pick up on and follow these cues. Silence is used as an invitation, a reprimand, a break and, sometimes, an ending. Knowing the difference between types of silence requires paying attention to the words other people are saying and their body language. People value someone who can listen effectively and navigate the barriers of silence.

This chapter will discuss techniques you can use to actively listen and why active listening is a desirable skill. We will also examine different types of silence, how to recognise them and how to respond to them.

Let Them Talk

Above all else, when interacting with others, people want to be heard. Feeling that your opinions are heard and understood helps reassure you that your ideas are real and valid. Humans are innately social, and listening to one another establishes the connections needed for successful interactions.

Each person sees a situation from their own unique perspective, which forms their opinions and views on a variety of subjects. This difference in view is what can create a diverse conversation or a difficult one. To make people feel heard during interactions, a person should remember to consider the other person's point of view before forming their own opinions or responding combatively. Remaining open to other people's ideas is the first step in hearing what they're saying and valuing the information. When someone can do this, it often makes the speaker feel validated and connected.

Just like loneliness can create health problems, engaging in daily conversation can have benefits for both physical and mental health. Conversation meets the psychological need to be social, which correlates with lower stress levels. Speaking out loud can help someone organise their thoughts if they have a lot on their plate and can improve memory overall. Speaking to others fosters a sense of community and can make people feel as if they belong to something bigger than themselves.

In addition to craving connection, humans have an innate desire for approval. Conversing with others can help fulfil this desire because it gives a person an opportunity to gain acceptance while receiving needed attention from others. Expressing ideas, especially with like-minded groups, can reinforce the idea that someone is appreciated for their interests and contributions, and this satisfies people's desire to be part of a community.

Conversations often make a person feel liked or understood by others, which can satisfy the need for societal approval. If their conversation partner is an effective listener, they may even receive feedback on how to improve their ideas. This collaboration can signal to the person that they are desired in return and help raise their self-esteem.

When people feel heard, they are typically more inclined to continue speaking and share more about themselves and thus continue the conversation. This is likely because their social needs are being met and they want to continue that feeling of approval and acceptance. The more intimate details you share with others, the closer to and more connected with them you will feel.

Although they may seem synonymous, hearing someone and listening to them are two very different tasks. Ironically, people feel heard when their conversational partner is effectively listening to them. Hearing is typically defined as simply picking up sound and processing its meaning. When a person hears someone, they are listening to the words, but not necessarily considering the meaning behind them.

Listening goes one step further. It includes taking in the words, considering the meaning behind them, and responding appropriately to the underlying context of the conversation. Listening often requires more concentration and attention to other factors, such as body language, to decipher the true meaning of a message.

Many people would like to be effective listeners to help their friends or colleagues work through difficult situations, but unfortunately, most people are naturally ineffective listeners. In fact, research shows people retain only 25–50 percent of what they hear. Given that small window, it is unlikely that a person would gather the most important information. Even if they were able to retain such important information, this large gap in attention might mean that they lack context for the information they have gathered, which could lead to misunderstandings.

Developing effective listening skills can help in social situations, personal relationships and work settings. If friends know someone is a good listener, they may be more inclined to speak to them regarding any issues or conflicts they are working through because they know their ideas will be heard. In personal relationships, listening is important because it makes a person more able to create effective compromises. At work, effective listening shows maturity and responsibility and makes it more likely a person will better collaborate on project with their team members.

An easy way for a person to show people they are paying attention is to employ active listening in conversation. This means using simple body language cues and consistent verbal feedback to signal they are listening to their conversational partner and considering their words. When someone listens actively, they are making a concerted effort to hear and retain all the information being presented. Using body language not only shows the partner that someone is listening but can also help reinforce the points in the listener's mind.

The basic tactics of active listening include nodding, taking notes and restating points to ensure clarity. These tactics all demonstrate understanding and open the opportunity for clarity in case there was a misunderstanding. By signalling that they are interested in the conversation, the person invites the speaker to ask if they have opinions or ideas to build on the topic being discussed.

Another key aspect of listening is waiting for silence, which can indicate a number of things in a conversation. One possibility is that the speaker is ready for their partner to jump into the speaking role. Understanding conversational silence and pauses relies on effective listening because a pause without context could be misinterpreted. If someone was not listening, they might interpret a pause to change topics as an opportunity to begin speaking, when it was not actually appropriate.

Waiting for the correct opening and respecting meaningful silence can show respect for the speaker. Listening carefully and not interrupting can make the speaker feel heard and important, whereas jumping in at the wrong time and potentially restating something already said could insult them.

Silence in a conversation could dictate the speed of

the interaction or be a nonverbal cue that something is wrong. Pauses in speech and the verbal pace of the conversation could often be a signal regarding how long the person intends to speak. Someone who pauses often to consider their words or speaks slowly may expect a more in-depth conversation with someone. Alternately, if someone is not pausing and speaking quickly, they are most likely signalling they do not plan on speaking for long.

Another use for silence can be to convey that something inappropriate was said. Especially in groups, when someone says something that is not generally accepted by the others, it is often met by silence. This is a type of negative reinforcement of the behaviour by not responding with positive verbal feedback. On the other hand, silence could be used to encourage further conversation. A good way to use silence to this end is to ask questions in a conversation and remain quiet until the other person is able to answer. Even if it takes some time for them to form a response, remaining silent demonstrates patience and a genuine interest in the answer.

Remaining silent while others are speaking can show them they will have the opportunity to state their opinions without being interrupted. This can foster more confidence in the speaker and help them resist the urge to edit their thoughts. This type of silence can demonstrate that a person wants to get to know their conversation partner beyond superficial small talk.

Body language during silence is an important way to communicate mood and receptiveness. When a person is postured openly, people receive that as being friendly and are more likely to feel comfortable approaching that person and sharing ideas. If someone is using open body language, they are more likely to have an open-ended conversation. On the other hand, if someone is closed off —arms crossed, looking down, blank face—people will feel more uneasy and be less likely to start a lengthy conversation.

The Power of Listening

A good listener is highly valued by others because, as discussed previously, being heard evokes a number of positive emotions in people. Having an effective listener as a conversational partner can show the speaker that someone understands their point of view. It is a way for the speaker to be seen in the light they would like to be seen in, instead of the many contexts people may view them in during the day. Another benefit of having someone listen is that it empowers people to continue sharing their ideas with others.

Being attentive will benefit the listener because it can help them solve complex problems, make difficult decisions and steer clear of conflicts with others. Active listening means a person is taking in considerable amounts of information and considering other viewpoints. It means they retain more of the information so their bank of resources for problem solving will be larger than those of others.

This plethora of information can help when someone needs to make a difficult decision. They will be able to consider the problem from multiple viewpoints, which can help someone determine their own feelings or examine situations they may not have considered. An active listener is likely to meet other people who are willing to take the time to reciprocate and listen to them. Having people willing to share their feedback can make difficult decisions a little easier.

When people practice empathy in listening, it makes it more likely they will react with compassion in difficult situations. Having this positive emotional reaction makes it easier for the person to avoid the conflict that might arise due to not considering another person's feelings. Hearing the other person out shows that you are willing to be patient so that the other person feels heard and valued. It also ensures a person will not accuse someone of anything inaccurate in the heat of the moment. Reacting with patience and empathy can help arguments remain calm and civilised.

In the event someone does end up in an argument,

listening can be the key to a successful resolution. Remembering not to immediately respond with emotion and hear the other person's view first can show that someone is willing to reach a resolution, instead of engaging in a screaming match. It gives a person an opportunity to respond with empathy once they are aware of how the other person is feeling.

The ability to effectively listen to others can have a major impact on someone's social success. Not being distracted by outside stimuli and giving feedback on someone's points demonstrate a willingness to focus on and contribute to the conversation. It shows the person that their ideas are being heard and valued, which makes them more likely to elaborate and ask for advice. It makes it easier for the listener to retain information if they are able to block out distractions and focus on the speaker, instead of what they are planning to say next.

While focusing on the conversation, it is important to restate anything that may seem confusing to clarify the information and ensure that there are no misunderstandings. This not only shows that a person is invested in understanding the information but also ensures they will not present it incorrectly to someone else. Giving the speaker an opportunity to clarify points shows that the listener is concerned with not only hearing their point of view but understanding it on a deeper level as well.

Asking broad questions to encourage the other

person to elaborate will ultimately provide a better idea of that other person's views. In this way, a person can react with empathy. Allowing someone to carry the conversation can give the listener more context about why someone might feel they way they do and teach them how to react if a similar situation arose in the future. Responding with empathy shows someone is considering the speaker's feelings, in addition to the information, which can help the speaker feel comfortable sharing more personal information.

4

USING YOUR EYES WHEN YOU SPEAK

S ome people may think that listening to others is a job for only their ears, but it is a task for their eyes as well. Looking for cues beyond people's words can help someone establish context and get to the root of the message, even if the person is not saying it directly. Making eye contact creates an intimate environment that can encourage someone to be more open with their conversational partner. It makes the conversation and the speaker more memorable. Looking at people for cues also includes using appearances to make statements. Most people are judged first by their appearance and second by their personality. Knowing how to dress appropriately and show the right message about the situation can lead to higher confidence. Finally, awkward situations can be the death of conversations unless the person knows what to look for to break the tension. If a person can see where the tension is coming from, it is considerably easier to dispel it and get a conversation back on track.

This chapter will discuss how to look for clues in people's posture when they are speaking and the benefits of making eye contact during conversations. We will go over how appearances can affect perception, how to handle diversity and how to diffuse an awkward situation.

Use Your Eyes

Much like listening and hearing are different activities, looking and seeing are also distinctive tasks based on how a person is responding to the information. Someone who is seeing something may not be receiving all the contextual information that the object they are looking at conveys. For example, if someone sees a stick in the ground, it is most likely in a passing glance, and they do not continue thinking about it. If someone is looking at the stick, however, they may stop walking to bend over and examine it so they can draw conclusions about why it fell or how it got there. Looking at something means taking in information and using that to form thoughts or opinions.

Looking at a person's qualities instead of seeing their appearance can help someone find a way to connect with them and understand them better. When doctors see their patients, they will look at the way the patient is feeling and see the test results to put together a hypothesis. Looking for the feeling behind people's words can give context to their conversation and help someone react more appropriately than if they weren't looking for such cues. Speakers will notice when their conversational partner is looking at them, instead of being distracted, and are often encouraged to continue being open.

Part of looking is making eye contact during a conversation. This is a great way to use nonverbal communication to connect with others and show that someone is truly paying attention to the speaker. Eye contact has been shown to make conversations more memorable for the listener and help people remember the speaker later. It is a great way to bridge the gap between hearing and listening by engaging the other person in the conversation. Making eye contact encourages people to be honest and makes them more aware of themselves, which makes them more conscientious conversational partners.

Making eye contact can be nerve-wracking for some, though, because it demonstrates a certain level of intimacy not everyone is comfortable with. If a person is uncomfortable making eye contact in conversations, there are a few ways they can work their way up to it. Practicing eye contact on video calls, for example, is a way to get a feel for the activity while still using a buffer zone so that it is not quite so intimate. When confronted with a real-life conversation, if someone cannot bring themselves to make eye contact, they can try looking at a spot near the other person's eyes without looking directly into them. This makes the other person think their listener is making eye contact and often produces similar benefits.

If someone is looking at a speaker in conversation, they may notice that most people have a persona they put on when speaking to others. Most people have a personal self and a social self, which is what they present to the world. Often times, the social self seems more put together and in control than a person feels that they actually are. This mask helps them feel more appealing, but a skilled onlooker can detect cracks in the mask. No one wants to present an alternate persona all the time, so if a listener can give them an opportunity to shed the mask, it can lead to trust between the two people.

Although most people will not say it, there is an underlying understanding in society that everyone wants to be heard, seen, and valued. People offer opinions to groups to feel included and connected to others. If they feel they don't quite fit in, they may put on a social mask to make themselves more appealing to the group. By creating a persona they think is more likely to be accepted, they may feel they have solidified a chance to feel valuable to a community.

Masks are not always worn to make someone more desirable, though. Some people wear their masks as a deterrent, hoping to keep others away so they do not have to face their own insecurities. These masks can be things such as anger, irritability, or rudeness, anything that helps to keep other people from connecting with them. This could be because they are terrified that, if they show their true self to someone, that person might be unimpressed or uninterested. Often, masks of deterrence are a self-preservation tactic and a way to refrain from being vulnerable to others.

Despite how scary it may be, if someone can manage to take their mask off, it can be an incredibly rewarding experience. When they take off their mask, a person can experience relief from the constant effort it takes to keep up a persona for others and keep track of how to act in front of which groups. It gives them an opportunity to realise that people will accept them for who they are without having to put on a show. This positive reinforcement of vulnerability often leads to increased self-confidence and self-esteem.

Look Behind the Curtain

Despite the adage "Don't judge a book by its cover", people often form first impressions based on appearance before speaking to someone. Therefore, it's important for people to dress the way they want people to see them. If someone's wardrobe is organised and neatly pressed, most people will perceive that person as organised and in control. The converse is true as well.

Facial cues play a large role in people's perceptions of others. A smile and open body posture show that someone is friendly and open to new ideas and can encourage others to approach them and start a conversation. Alternately, frowning or blank faces and a closed off body posture, such as crossed arms, can give people a "leave me alone" message that may keep them from approaching.

Studies have shown that appearance can even determine what you are paid at your job. A 2004 study performed by Timothy Judge at the University of Florida showed that tall people are paid almost $800 more than their shorter competitors. Another study from George Washington University showed that overweight people are paid significantly less than average-weight people. Others studies showed that even trivial attributes, such as hair colour, physical fitness and wearing makeup, can affect a person's pay rate.

With this in mind, it is important for people to be aware of how they are presenting themselves in a business setting. Dressing professionally could mean the difference between a moderate salary and a substantial raise. In a business setting, people need to make sure their clothes fit well and are free of wrinkles, tears, blemishes and stains. Sleek lines and simple colours are preferred to bright patterns. It can be a good idea for someone to always have a suit on hand in case they are pulled into a board meeting; in that case, they will still have appropriate attire. This level of judgement doesn't feel nice to hear; it is wrong and discriminatory, but sadly, it does happen, so being aware of how you present yourself in specific social circles can make a big difference in how easy your conversations are.

Your personal style can be given a little more leeway in the sense that people can express themselves in terms of colours and materials but should still remember that others will be using appearance to make judgments. Some simple rules you can follow to be sure you are presenting an appealing image are to dress for the occasion and always look like you put some effort into your appearance. For example, wearing pyjamas to the grocery store — no matter what time — doesn't show that a person put effort into what they were wearing and suggests an image of being a sloth. Smart jeans and a designer t-shirt, however, show that the person cared enough about their own image to want others to think they look good as well.

Just like everyone has their own personal style, people have different personalities and communication styles. Part of interacting is embracing people's differences and working with them to expand personal talents and abilities. When speaking with someone different from yourself, you should make an effort to use empathy and understand things from the other person's perspective. It is worth noting that accepting someone for their differences and being open-minded does not mean a person has to agree with them. Part of overcoming differences is being able to have discussions about things people disagree on.

In the event someone has never encountered diversity or does not know how to handle it, there are three things they can remember to be respectful and try to understand the other person. First, a person should always be aware that most social situations are made up of diverse people who all have different ideas and backgrounds. Beyond this, though, these people will all have similarities as well. A person attempting to bridge this diversity gap can search for similarities between themselves and the other person to establish a common ground they can then move forward from.

The next thing to remember is that, in almost all diversity situations, there is something to learn from the other person. Asking questions about differences can help someone understand a culture or set of beliefs that are different from their own and allow them to proceed in a respectful manner. They may be able to relate some of their own views to those of the other person. It is usually a better practice to ask and learn than to assume and get information wrong.

Finally, sometimes, interacting with other people may require a specific skill, such as knowing a foreign language. In these situations, a person may need to use an interpreter or help the other person understand their own language using techniques other than verbal conversation.

Interacting with someone who is staunchly different can sometimes cause anxiety when a person is trying to find a common topic to discuss. A person should remember to be brave and confident in these situations. If they are making the effort to understand the other person's differences, they may even be able to find meaningful information in that discussion. If the root of the anxiety is a fear of saying something incorrect or offensive, then a person should ask questions about the topics they are unsure of to ensure they do not upset the other person unintentionally.

Most interactions have the potential to become awkward for several reasons. If a skilled conversationalist knows how to address the elephant in the room, however, they can easily dissipate the tension. Unfortunately, sometimes, the elephant in the room may be the person themselves, and the best way to dismiss this kind of tension is to acknowledge your own shortcomings. For example, if someone is attempting to speak to a socially awkward person and they are consistently answering with short, terse sentences, the initiator may think they are being rude, and the room could become tense. In this situation, the anxious person could simply try to continue the conversation and show they are interested in the interaction.

When the tension is coming from someone else, a person should gauge the situation by looking for facial cues and body language before stepping in. Sometimes, a conversation fizzles out, and there is a moment of pause before the group disperses. This is a natural occurrence at the end of an interaction and does not necessarily warrant intervention. If someone has just said something that was met with silence, crossed arms, and people distancing themselves, it may be time to hop in and lighten the mood by moving the conversation to a more acceptable topic.

There are many reasons an interaction can go stale, and most centre around a lack of communication between strangers, which can make approaching someone new especially intimidating. A person may feel particularly awkward when they enter a room where they don't know anyone else. This might make them wary regarding what topics are acceptable, so they might remain silent or unsuccessfully attempt to enter conversations. Accidentally entering another person's personal space can create an awkward situation. Most people have their personal boundary, and they like it to remain unoccupied in order to feel comfortable speaking to others. When someone invades this space, it can make the person feel uncomfortable.

Luckily, there are a variety of techniques you can use to diffuse awkward situations, such as what was mentioned previously. You can ask questions to try to find a common interest between the people in the conversation so that there is a topic that everyone can contribute to. It is easy to diffuse awkward situations by simply helping others, either with a problem you see them having or with getting away from the awkward comment they just made. One last attempt to clear the awkwardness can be simply pointing it out. Sometimes, showing people they are allowed to laugh at whatever happened is enough to ease the tension and open the conversation again.

5

STARTING A CONVERSATION

Conversation is an art form, and without the correct set of paints, someone's masterpiece can quickly become a disaster. The first brush stroke in painting a conversation is finding a way to introduce yourself to a group or another individual. Knowing how and when to insert an opinion into a conversation can be the determining factor in whether it is accepted. Easy conversation starters and comments can be a simple starting point for people looking to join an interaction. Focusing on other people helps them open up and feel more comfortable with sharing information. A person can do this by asking about their hobbies or interests. In addition to knowing how to start a conversation, a person should know how to end one—or rather how not to end one. Over-using compliments is a way to make people wary of interacting with someone because they may be seen as untrustworthy or inauthentic. There is a limit on how many compliments you can give before you are seen as sucking up to someone, which is never a good look.

This chapter discusses various ways a person can introduce themselves when joining a group conversation and easy statements that can get a conversation moving. This chapter looks at different ways to start and sustain small talk with others in a variety of situations. Finally, it will discuss the ways a person may unintentionally end a conversation and how to avoid compliments being misinterpreted as having an ulterior motive.

Keys to Conversation

Becoming part of an established conversation is one of the more difficult, but not impossible, tasks when attempting to expand your social skills. The key is to interject something meaningful and then take a step back to allow the group to receive you. This shows that a person has something to add to the conversation but does not want to dominate the group. It allows the other people in the group to evaluate what a person can contribute and make the decision to open the conversation to them, so the integration is as seamless as possible, which reduces awkwardness.

One way for a person to use this tactic is to be

assertive with their contribution. They can directly introduce themselves to the group and invite the speaker to
continue with their thoughts. This demonstrates to the
group that a person has no intention of coming in and
commanding the conversation. It shows a willingness to
be a listener, as well as a speaker, which is more likely to
gain approval from others, who may see a new person as
a threat to the conversational flow. The direct approach
can signal confidence, which may encourage others to
pursue one-on-one conversations with the person.

Another, less assertive way to join a conversation is to
wait patiently next to the group until a member invites
you. Waiting patiently establishes your presence and
being near the group shows you are interested in what
they are discussing. In some circles, waiting to be invited
into the conversation may be seen as the more polite
approach. Some people do not like others interrupting
the conversation, but when an established group member
brings in a new person, there is a dynamic of acceptance.
If the group is only loosely formed, then small talk with
members can be a good way to ease yourself into the
discussion.

Small talk can serve as a steppingstone to feeling
comfortable in large-group situations. It gives a person an
experience of starting simple conversations with people
and building on impromptu topics. Small talk can sometimes seem more difficult because it is one on one, but

there is more room for improvement in the early stages of conversation because a person is only dealing with one other person's feedback. It gives a person more opportunities to ask questions and learn about the best ways to phrase questions and what may be a difficult question for someone to answer.

Another benefit of small talk is that it can happen with anyone, so a person can gain valuable experience interacting with strangers. It can happen at water-coolers, in line at the grocery store or coffee shop or even on the bus during someone's daily commute. Simply having the confidence to approach others can be the difference between a great talk on the way to work and a silent bus ride. There are opportunities to interact with people everywhere, and small talk is a great way to take advantage of them.

Keeping it simple is often preferable to launching into deep conversations, especially with someone you don't know very well. Starting a conversation with personal information or a controversial topic can make the other person feel awkward or uncomfortable. Small talk is valuable for measuring where someone's conversational boundaries are and thus not overstepping them.

This method of easing into conversations helps build trust and connection between the conversational partners. It allows both parties to decide when they feel comfortable sharing more personal information and creates organic opportunities to do so. Sometimes, easing in takes place over multiple conversations and not all at once, but it still accomplishes the same goals.

If a person is struggling to find a topic to use in beginning small talk, they should think of something unique and casual to ask the other person to get the ball rolling. After introducing yourself and disposing of pleasantries, a person can ask about where a person grew up or what plans they're excited about that week. These questions not only make someone more memorable but also move the speaker into an open position, in which they can share more about themselves.

If someone is looking for more than just small talk, then inquiring about a person's interests or hobbies can be a great go-to in starting a conversation. Most people enjoy talking about themselves and the things that interest them, so it is a safe bet that these questions will start a robust conversation. Although it may seem like an obvious tactic, people will usually take any opportunity to discuss their interests with others. It can be especially lucky if someone's interests align with the inquirer's because then, they are able to contribute to the conversation and offer their own opinions. With luck, the two may form a friendship through the shared interest.

Some people don't give off signals that they want to be spoken to, but they may not realise they are shooing away potential conversational partners. For example, if someone is reading a book, a person could sit down next to them and ask what the book is about. If the reader responds positively, the person could then ask them to describe the plot. If there is no obvious introduction to the conversation, the person could start by sharing information about themselves. Not all people are immediately receptive to small talk, and a person may need to employ some icebreakers to lighten the mood and make the other person feel more comfortable sharing information about themselves. Everyone has experienced the corny icebreaker games teachers make them play in high school to learn about the class. These games are not always a good fit for adult situations, however, and other types of icebreakers may need to be used. These can be comments, observations or questions, but they are generally easy to answer and encourage the person to look up at the speaker and acknowledge their comment. Examples of icebreakers are sharing fun facts about yourself — if there are any you find particularly interesting — or pointing out something out of the ordinary happening in the immediate area. The latter especially encourages the person to look up from whatever they are doing and acknowledge the comment, which can easily lead to a conversation.

"Dad jokes" or corny puns are another way to strike up a conversation when the other person approaches first. If the person says, "Oh, your shoe is untied," then someone could respond, "No, I'm Bill." Making a joke out of a passing comment is a way to relax the other person and show them you are not intimidating or rude. This joke is a clean transition into introductions, and that is a natural start to any conversation.

There are many tactics someone can use to start a conversation, but it is typically a good idea to keep it light and funny if possible. Putting people at ease before an interaction is an art-form, but with practice, most people can achieve it. It's all about reading the visual cues, waiting for the right time and choosing an easy topic to discuss with anyone. These skills are the building blocks of successful small talk.

How to Kill a Conversation

The contrary art to starting conversations is abruptly ending them. Even the most organic conversations are subject to certain comments or subjects that sour people's moods and end the exchange. These comments are not always intentional, so it is helpful to be aware of what they are so a person does not accidentally kill a good conversation.

One sure way to kill a conversation is to add negative feedback. Part of interacting with others is providing feedback to help solve a problem or contribute to a difficult situation. This positive exchange of ideas is what draws people to conversations and social interactions; it is what promotes the positive psychological effects and social fulfilment people derive from conversation. Adding negative feedback in a positive environment can turn everyone's mood quickly and make them not want to discuss the topic further. It is an easy way for someone to show others they are not interested in solving problems or collaborating in a group.

A second way to unintentionally end a conversation is to constantly point out faux pas or mistakes the other people make. If someone misspeaks and it does not change their message, it does no good to point out their mistakes in front of others. This is a type of negative feedback. It makes people think too much about what they will say and if it is correct instead of focusing on what they are trying to say. Forcing people to edit themselves when they speak does not promote an open and friendly environment. Often, if someone constantly points out others' mistakes, then people will stop speaking with them to avoid the negative feedback.

Most people don't want to contribute negatively to a conversation, so they might turn to compliments as a way to positively reinforce their place in a group or be invited into a conversation. It is well-known that people enjoy hearing compliments; it can boost self-esteem and confidence and make someone feel appreciated and liked. These results are the reason some people choose to use compliments as a way into groups. This tactic, however, can turn bad quickly if someone does not know how to walk the line between complimenting someone and sucking up to them with too much flattery, which can make people feel awkward, especially if this over-use of flattery is directed toward the opposite sex.

Compliments show someone has an interest in a topic or person and demonstrates that they would like to be included in a discussion, either currently or in the future. An effective compliment makes other people want to include someone in their interactions. It sticks with people, so they always remember that the person is interested in a particular topic. Effective compliments match positive feelings with a certain person, which makes it more likely people will include them in the future. As previously mentioned, though, compliments should not be doled out uncontrollably. There is a fine line in terms of when compliments become suspicious, and people may think the speaker is only out to gain something. People who overtly flatter others are generally not trusted and can have more difficulty joining groups. Therefore, knowing how many compliments are enough is imperative.

It may be difficult to determine whether frequent compliments are leading into awkward territory. In these situations, a person can examine the type and frequency of compliments to be sure their words are not mistaken for over-flattery. Since knowing when to stop can be the difference between acceptance and the cold shoulder, it is important to remember that there are a few ways to keep compliments in check. One way concerns itself more with complimenting people, and the other is focused on compliments in general.

When complimenting people, too frequent praise can be interpreted as trying to gain favour, especially if the person being complimented is a boss or superior. Keeping compliments to a minimum when it comes to superficial observations, such as someone's appearance, is typically best practice. You should never find yourself searching for something to compliment. Good qualities speak for themselves and do not need to be sought out to praise. Complimenting someone every day can grow tedious for both parties and is often eventually perceived as needless flattery. If a person simply saves compliments for genuine moments, then they can usually stay in the safe zone.

6

THE CONTEXT OF A CONVERSATION

Interacting with others can stir up a lot of feelings in a person, good and bad. These feelings can be dictated by what is said, who the speaker is speaking with, or even the environment they are in. Conversational environments can include both physical space and emotional setting and have a considerable impact on the success of an interaction. Along with the environment, the overall context of the conversation is also important. Context can mean the difference between talking about running home from work or running home from third base on the baseball field. Depending on when someone comes into a conversation, they may not have enough information to understand that the group is discussing a baseball game and not a marathon runner. Context can come from visual cues or emotional signals showing how a person might react to a particular subject. When people do not have the correct context, they may jump to conclusions about the information someone is providing. Even with the proper context, sometimes, people spend more energy attempting to piece information together than attempting to retain it all. This can lead to people missing important information and not paying adequate attention to a speaker. When conclusions are drawn, assumptions are often made as well. Assumptions take conclusions one step further because, when people assume, they decide their conclusions are true and act on them as facts. Making assumptions can be harmful to relationships and should never be done without first seriously considering whether the information one has is true.

This chapter will discuss various types of conversational environments and how a person can identify them. It will talk about how to act in various environments to maintain the status quo and not create an awkward situation. Then, we will move to how context contributes to conversations and how to notice context before starting a conversation. Finally, we will examine how drawing conclusions and making assumptions can be harmful to interactions and relationships.

Understand the Situation and Reading the Room

People react and adapt to their environments in many ways, including how they communicate. To have a successful interaction with someone, it is important to take the social environment into account before deciding on how to approach the conversation. The environment of a conversation can be determined by considering a few factors. The location, for example, can determine the volume and intimacy of the conversation. How many people are included in the conversation can create an environment for certain kinds of discussions that everyone can participate in. Being aware of the environment helps a person avoid making mistakes or social faux pas.

One example of a delicate conversational environment would be if someone joined a support group for people with social anxiety. Because the group exists to encourage the members to overcome fears, this would be an inappropriate place for negative feedback or interrupting others. Another consideration when determining the environment is the volume of a conversation. As mentioned, some group conversations can get rowdy, and people may start yelling just to be heard over others. If someone is in a quiet place, though, such as a library or office, speaking too loudly may be inappropriate for the setting.

Conversations alone can even create an environment with the words people choose and the tone of the speakers. This is a type of emotional environment that people should be aware of when deciding how to respond to people. If people are discussing their feelings or vulnerabilities, they most likely think they are in a safe, relaxed environment free of judgement. A person walking into that situation should notice the delicacy of the emotional environment and respect the person speaking by actively listening and offering caring feedback.

Not all emotional environments are positive, though. Sometimes, a person may find themselves in an angry or judgmental environment. For example, if someone is sitting in a meeting at work and the boss begins to reprimand a co-worker in front of everyone, this can create a negative emotional environment. People may be reluctant to speak up because they see the boss is angry and do not want to be included in the negative back and forth. These situations are not always so straightforward, so looking for signs of stress, such as clenched fists or gritted teeth, can give a clue that you are walking into a negative emotional environment.

There are some key things a person can do to ensure they are promoting a healthy, happy conversational environment. The first is to establish the emotional environment as a safe place by encouraging trust and honesty by using open body language and eye contact, which can demonstrate to others that a person is willing to interact in a positive environment. This can make people feel more comfortable sharing their feelings because they do not have to fear judgment or negative critiques.

Another way to promote a positive environment is to be accepting of people's ideas and willing to discuss them with an open mind. When others know, they will not have to walk on eggshells in a conversation, it can encourage them to elaborate on ideas and continue the conversation. A person can build on this by showing appreciation for the other person opening up and offering helpful feedback. To show appreciation, someone can recognise when the speaker makes valid points or use active listening techniques, such as nodding or verbally agreeing with what is being said. People who feel appreciated in a conversation are often inclined to speak with their conversational partner again in the future.

Just as social interactions are dictated by their environment, they can be dictated by the context surrounding them. Context is similar to environment because it can be both physical and emotional, but context goes a little deeper than just what is going on in a conversation. Context explores the meaning of the environment and social cues. A person can find context in facial cues, body language, or asking someone about an observed difference. Knowing the context of a conversation can ensure someone knows how to proceed without offending their partner or being perceived as rude. Sometimes, there are multiple layers of context, but a person can typically rely on what they can pick up on their own to get started in a conversation.

Facial expressions are an easy way to gain context regarding how someone feels about the topic being discussed. If their face is relaxed and they are making eye contact with the speaker, they are probably interested in the topic. If their face is in a grimace or frown or they refuse to look at the speaker, however, they probably disapprove of with either the topic or the speaker's opinions on it. Some facial cues are even more subtle, such as a furrowed brow, someone touching their face or eyes darting around the room. A furrowed brow usually shows frustration or confusion and often means a person is working through a problem on their own.

Keeping an eye on body language, which often goes together with facial expressions, is another way to track conversational context. Open posture, such as leaving one's arms at one's side or sitting facing the crowd, show someone is willing to engage in a conversation. Closed postures, such as crossed arms or sitting facing the wall, are typically signs someone is not interested in speaking with others.

Context can be social or cultural differences within a group, which may change the way the group members perceive or understand information. For example, if an American gave a thumbs-up to someone from the Middle East and that person got upset, the American might become confused. Without the context that a thumbs-up is a rude gesture in some Middle Eastern cultures, an American may offend the other person. Communication disorders, such as hearing loss, can be a barrier to interaction without context. If someone is aware they are speaking to someone with profound hearing loss, they can compensate by using hand gestures or sign language to properly convey their message.

Take Your Time

When interacting with others, it is basic human nature to make inferences from the information we receive, but these inferences may not always be based on fact. People tend to jump to conclusions when they receive information, and this can sometimes even keep them from hearing all of the information. Conclusions drawn from speculation are seldom accurate and can even damage relationships when a person becomes upset about a conclusion they've made. This is why it is important to always consider information rationally and logically before forming a conclusion or opinion about someone or something.

If a person is in a conversation and they are not sure

of something or notice themselves starting to draw conclusions based on incomplete information, a simple fix is to ask the other person to clarify their meaning. This gives the speaker an opportunity to give needed background or additional information that can provide more context for the situation. Conclusions are often drawn when a person does not have the proper context, so remembering tricks with which to gain context can help with gathering information.

When someone is presenting copious amounts of information at once, a person should remember to be patient and wait until the speaker is finished to draw conclusions. Making assumptions halfway through someone giving information is a sure way to get the wrong idea. A good trick to avoid falling into this trap is to actively listen to people. When a person employs the skills used in active listening, they are more focused on the words and the meanings behind them than their own thoughts. This means they do not have time to come up with conclusions while the speaker is talking because they are busy taking in information. After letting the other person finish, you can then take time to put the pieces together and draw an informed conclusion.

Part of drawing an accurate conclusion means breaking down the parts of a person's spoken information into manageable chunks. It can be tempting to glaze over parts of a conversation that were difficult to understand, but this can mean missing key pieces of information. If a person can be patient with the way they process information, they will typically be less likely to draw inaccurate conclusions.

Jumping to conclusions is especially easy for people with social anxiety because their discomfort during conversations can cause their mind to race and make it difficult to focus on the speaker for the entire duration of a conversation. As discussed in Chapter Two, people with social anxiety can have trouble regulating self-criticism. This sometimes leads to them bracing themselves in conversation for a blow they're sure is coming. For example, someone with social anxiety may interpret someone with a direct conversation style as being forceful and conclude that this person does not like them. They may draw the conclusion that the person is rude and thinks they're stupid, but this is not based on rational information.

For people who find themselves in this situation, it can be helpful to take a moment to mentally step back from the situation and assess it without the emotions getting in the way. If a person can look at the entire picture, not just their own interpretation of the situation, they are more likely to draw a rational conclusion as compared to an emotional one. Part of learning from this process is acknowledging how the initial conclusion was incorrect and how to adjust one's thought process in the future.

In line with not rushing to conclusions, people should avoid making assumptions based on their inferences. An assumption is when someone draws a conclusion from the information they have and decide it is a fact, even though they may not have all the information. This goes one step further than a conclusion by treating something that has not been confirmed as true, as if it is an undeniable fact.

Assumptions can be detrimental to relationships, both intimate and friendly. Assumptions can lead to accusations, which can shatter the trust two people have between one another. To ensure they are not making assumptions, a person should follow a similar procedure as in attempting not to draw conclusions. Take a step back from the situation and ask what evidence there is that a given idea is a fact. If a person cannot trace the information back to the speaker or another undeniable source, then it is most likely an assumption.

People need to try to notice the difference between facts and assumptions and therefore keep open lines of communication. If a person refrains from assuming and instead asks for clarity, they are more likely to obtain accurate information. This encourages further conversation and interaction with others and shows that the person is a trustworthy friend. Refraining from making assumptions allows people to stay away from unwanted conflict and unintended offence. If an assumption is incorrect and someone tells it to others, they could potentially be harming another person's reputation. If they accuse someone of something they didn't do based on an assumption, it could lead to losing that person in their life over something silly. Simply asking questions to clarify confusing information or situations can keep a person away from assuming and potentially harming others.

It can be difficult to retrain our brains to stop making assumptions, so being aware of the process and making efforts to change it are key to stopping this practice. When a person notices themselves making an assumption, they should remember to shift from their perspective to that of the speaker. Sometimes, thinking about a situation from someone else's point of view can provide some clarity. It can help a person consider the meaning of a speaker's words and how they feel about the information. They should remember to think through the information and process it logically, not emotionally, to find the facts within and draw a likely conclusion.

7

COURTESY AND RESPECT

Establishing relationships with people is one thing, but keeping those relationships is another task entirely. To grow relationships, a person needs to know how to treat others with courtesy, kindness and respect. This includes always preserving their dignity and honouring other people's boundaries. Most people have physical boundaries, which are understood rather than stated, but some have emotional boundaries. Not everyone likes to discuss personal information, and those boundaries should be respected. As in every situation, people should remember that empathy is king in social interactions. Thinking about another person's feelings before reacting is a sure recipe for being kind and courteous. When a person is empathetic, it can be easy to build bridges with others who may not seem to have obvious similarities. Once the bridge is built, the person can then proceed to start chipping away at any walls another person may have up to guard themselves or their information. This process should always be done slowly and respectfully. Finally, not everyone is perfect, and sometimes, people will hurt the feelings of others. No one should be discouraged by this, however. Learning to forgive and move on from difficult situations can further solidify a relationship.

This chapter discusses how courtesy can positively affect an interaction and provides a few ways for a person to ensure they are being courteous. It examines the different types of boundaries and how to recognise when a person's boundaries are being challenged. It looks at empathy as a way to build relationships and establish common ground from which to start a conversation. Finally, this chapter looks at breaking through barriers to get to know someone, and why it is important to forgive people and move on.

How to Treat Others

People say "You catch more flies with honey than with vinegar" for a reason. It is easier to make social advances when you are courteous to someone than when you are grumpy and rude because the former demonstrates respect. When strangers act with courtesy, smile at others or do someone a favour, it often evokes a positive reaction from the other person. These acts can make a person feel appreciated, respected and valued — all things people that make people happy. On the other hand, if a stranger is rude to someone, grimaces at them or refuses to help them, this can elicit a negative response from the other person. This is because the stranger is neglecting basic common courtesy and may even seem as if they are going out of their way to be rude.

People respond positively to politeness and etiquette because they are typically raised to respect people with good manners. It shows compassion toward others, which is a basic building block of any functioning society. Acting with compassion can demonstrate trustworthiness and encourage people to want to interact with someone. Etiquette shows the other person they will not be dominated in an interaction and their conversation partner is aware of how to be polite when someone is expressing their ideas.

The key to being courteous is to always remember the most important thing in any interaction is to preserve the dignity of both parties. Manners mean having the sense not to embarrass someone needlessly or start a conflict in an inappropriate environment. Although it can be easy to get caught up in emotions, people should always try to wait until they do not feel emotional about an issue to bring it up to someone else. This will make sure they do not approach the problem in a way they might regret later, such as yelling at co-workers in the office.

Another aspect of being courteous to a conversational partner is respecting their boundaries. All interactions have both verbal and nonverbal boundaries that a person should be aware of and respect. One way to keep tabs on the physical boundaries in an interaction is to remember the communication theory termed proxemics.

Proxemics is a theory that states the distance a person stands from the other person in a conversation is directly related to the intimacy level of both the conversation and the two parties. The more personal a conversation is, the closer someone is likely to stand to their friend. The less personal a conversation is, the more space there will be. This relates to how well the two people know one another. If two strangers were having a conversation, it would be unlikely they'd be standing close enough to touch one another, just as if a student was talking to a teacher in the classroom. If two good friends were speaking to one another, however, they would likely stand close together.

Boundaries can be emotional or mental; some people are more open with others in general, and other people prefer to keep their personal information private. Usually, people will use body language, or nonverbal cues, to signal whether they are willing to discuss personal infor-mation with someone. When a personal subject is brought up, if the person begins to show closed body language, they are probably not comfortable discussing the topic, and the speaker may be approaching a boundary. Some people may even directly tell a person they are crossing a boundary. In both situations, the speaker must recognise they are making the other person uncomfortable, apologise and change the subject to something more acceptable.

Some people may put up boundaries that seem unnecessary or aggressive. It can be off-putting to feel like someone is initially unapproachable, but this is a great opportunity to use empathy to get someone to open up. Sometimes, people establish boundaries to avoid talking about something difficult or painful for them, so understanding why the boundary exists is the first step to helping the person adjust it. For example, if a person casually asked how someone was liking the weather and they responded with a snide comment, this could be a sign that this person has very strict boundaries and probably does not want to interact with anyone. If someone were to consistently show compassion to this person, however, they might eventually be willing to participate in small talk and eventually a full conversation. Understanding that such anger may be coming from within and not be directed at anyone in particular can help the person persist despite the negative feedback.

Providing an understanding environment through

empathy is a great way to make people feel at ease. When someone feels understood, they are often more likely to share their problems with someone else because they know they will not be judged. This can be a lengthy process, however; trust is not developed over night. People must be ready to have a consistent empathetic mindset and continue showing others they are willing to talk if the other person desires. This unrelenting empathy helps to dissolve boundaries and forge meaningful relationships.

When a person is courteous, respects boundaries and acts empathetically, they can open a plethora of conversational doors for themselves. These qualities are what help ease the initial tension of new interactions and can even promote interaction beyond the initial conversation. Every person wants to be respected and have their boundaries respected and acknowledged as well. In addition, people generally treat others with courtesy and expect the same in return. If someone can master doing this while being sympathetic to the other person's point of view, it will likely be easy to start conversations with anyone.

How to Build Relationships

Beyond empathy and courtesy, there are many ways to foster a connection with other people and build relationships. One way is to focus on positive sentiments and work toward compromises instead of embracing conflict. People generally respond well to a positive disposition because it can be a helpful way to dispel stress and distract from other problems in their lives. Working toward compromise shows a willingness to collaborate and focus on outcomes that are beneficial for everyone. This can signal selflessness and kindness to others. Including everyone in a group conversation is another way to demonstrate kindness and can keep cliques from forming within a group. Including everyone is a way to build collaboration and loop in more people who can help in reaching compromises.

Another way to demonstrate selflessness is by trying to understand the other person before offering comments. Considering an issue from the other person's perspective is not only respectful but also allows a person to consider more options for compromise if the discussion needs a resolution. When a person allows the speaker to voice their opinions first, they may be able to clear up a question before having to voice it at all.

Another important factor is keeping information private after the conversation has finished. Especially when someone shares personal information in a conversation, it is typically in bad taste to share that information with others. When people are vulnerable, there is an established trust between the parties that the information will not go further than their conversation. Breaching this trust usually results in people not wanting to open up to that person anymore.

Some people rebel against even the most polite attempts to social build bridges, though. They may hide behind one-word answers and brief conversations to keep conversations and interactions at bay. At this point, a person should be able to notice closed body language and recognise the driving force behind it. Despite how aloof a person may seem, there are ways to break down conversational walls and get to the heart of such a person.

One way is to ask follow-up questions to keep the person talking. The more they speak, the more they will likely become comfortable with the conversation. Even if the questions only warrant one-word answers, it can still be helpful for the person to interact at any level. The more they speak, the more they will be able to realise that whatever negativity they might have expected is not going to occur, which will reassure them as they continue. When attempting to break down barriers, it is crucial that a person takes off their social mask and presents their true self. Being vulnerable with others encourages them to be vulnerable with us, and it can serve as an olive branch in a difficult interaction. Really knowing a person encourages someone to expose their true selves as well.

Not everyone will adhere to the social rules of interaction and conversation, though, and sometimes, this can lead to a person having their feelings hurt or becoming upset with the offender. To create a truly meaningful relationship, a person must be able to forgive someone for missteps, intentional or not, and move on from them. No one is perfect, and most people do not intentionally offend other people. If someone is having trouble forgiving another person, they can try to be empathetic and imagine how the other person may be feeling. This is usually enough for someone to understand why the person said what they did and how they might be feeling guilty or regretful.

Part of forgiving someone is being merciful. If they seem to regret the offence but are not reaching out to clear the air, it can be a good idea for someone to reach out with forgiveness before the other person offers an apology. Sometimes, being the bigger person is the best way to move on from a hurtful situation.

Finally, the most important part of forgiveness is forgetting. Don't let the offence linger after forgiving someone. People need to know that when they are forgiven, they will no longer be persecuted or judged for the offence. This is an integral step for both parties to move on.

8

KEEPING CONVERSATION LIGHT AND THE POWER OF LAUGHTER

Even though someone might want to have a deep conversation with another person, it is typically best practice to keep things light at first. Starting with small talk about a simple subject and working up to more personal topics can be an easy way to interact with new people and get them to trust you. Keeping the conversation light and casual lowers the odds that a person may offend someone with an off-the-cuff comment or joke. Additionally, people should remember to see the good in others. It can be easy to immediately notice the negative qualities in someone and use that to form an opinion. If someone can take a moment to notice the positive qualities, though, it can make the conversation much more productive. It can also help a person to see the good in themselves.

When someone is interacting with a new social group, they can benefit from keeping an open mind and allowing the other person to express their opinions. Sometimes, people are met with ideas that are very different from their own and remaining open can be a challenge. It can be helpful to remember that the goal of a conversation is not to start an argument but to collaborate with others and share ideas. The key to not responding negatively to new ideas is to keep the emotions in check, stay present in the conversation and not be afraid to leave your comfort zone.

People can even call attention to their own shortcomings as a light-hearted way to jump into conversation. Self-deprecating humour — when executed properly — can boost a person's self-esteem and confidence. It shows others they are not too concerned with their own image to have a little fun.

This chapter discusses why people should try to keep conversations light and fun when initiating interactions, especially with strangers. We look at how people can take a step back to find the good in others, as well as how that can positively contribute to the conversation and a group. It explains why people should remain open-minded when confronted with new ideas and how self-deprecating humour can help create a light environment.

Keep it Light

Participating in small talk and starting a new conversation both depend on a certain light-heartedness from both parties to keep the mood positive. If someone dives into a heavy subject, it can kill the mood right away. Inversely, keeping things too light can sometimes lead to people thinking someone is not capable of a serious discussion. There is a delicate middle ground people must be able to tread to start quality conversations.

One important point to remember is that most people are inherently critical of themselves, some more than others. When trying to start a conversation with a new person, you should not rely on opportunities to poke fun at the person as an opener. Someone may accidentally call out a quality the other person is sensitive to and does not want other people to notice. This can make them upset before the conversation even begins and not want to engage socially.

This is not saying someone should not be offended when another person makes a passing joke at their expense. It is okay to feel upset when someone uses you as conversational fodder, but the trick to keeping the conversation going is not letting it bother you in the moment. Laugh at yourself so the conversation can continue and does not become awkward for the other members. Later, a person can address the offence privately with the offender so that they can explain the comment was not appreciated and ask them not to repeat it.

When approaching a new group, the best bet in starting a conversation is to pick a light topic that everyone can discuss. This can include a common experience, the weather (us Brits love talking about the weather), the commute to work or anything else that everyone is sure to have an opinion about. Asking about something common gives everyone a chance to participate and feel included. It keeps conversations light because no one will want to stray from a conversation that includes the whole group.

Another way to approach a light-hearted conversation is to ask the other person about themselves. This gives the person the opportunity to decide the topic and tone of the conversation, which ensures their comfort. If walking up to someone and asking what their favourite colour is seems strange, try using context to pick a good introduction. For example, if someone is drinking a coffee, you could ask them if it is a light or dark roast and then offer your favourite type of coffee. This simple conversation starter could easily lead to an in-depth examination of both parties' coffee preferences. Keeping conversations light like this opens the door to further conversation down the road.

Starting off simple increases a person's chances that

someone will not judge them negatively from the get-go. Although most people are wired to see the negative qualities in someone more quickly than the positives, it can be helpful to look for the good qualities in someone because it makes a person feel safer in their environment. Instead of drawing conclusions or making assumptions, a person should take time to notice the good qualities in someone, instead of racing to form a negative view of them based on a general impression. If someone steps back and considers the person as a whole, they can usually find a number of positive character traits.

Making a point to notice people's desirable qualities can get someone's brain trained to see the same qualities in themselves. Part of seeing the good in others is acknowledging it in yourself first. When people take time to discern what qualities they have that benefit others and decide to work on the qualities that don't, they are practicing discerning between negative and positive actions. This can translate to others, as well, and make the process of appreciating someone much easier.

Looking for the good in others can help create a sense of community in a group and help people overcome their differences and work together. Many people are influenced by their environment and the people around them. If they see other people doing nice things, this can make them want to do nice things as well. Passing along this kindness promotes compromise and collaboration, which can be a great foundation for a cohesive group. These good deeds might even eventually create a chain of kindness that builds interactions and relationships beyond the initial person or group.

The more good deeds a person does, the better sense of their own morality they have. Most people strive to be good people. They go out of their way to help others when they have the opportunity, and they actively try to make others feel happy and accepted. Sometimes, though, it can be difficult for a person to measure their own understanding of moral and immoral acts. If someone is consistently striving to be a model for others, they will likely be able to identify that their good deeds and good feelings correlate. This reinforces the idea that acting with compassion is moral and can benefit everyone involved.

Part of treating everyone with kindness may be meeting new people along the way. Meeting new people means being exposed to new ideas and opinions. When someone has ideas or opinions that don't match another person's, they should always approach the conversation with an open mind and do their best not to judge the other person. Part of interacting with new people is getting to know their viewpoint and background to better understand their perspective. Once a person understands someone's perspective, then they can lead the conversation into a respectful debate if they wish or simply treat the interaction as a learning experience.

People can learn a great deal by discussing problems or topics with someone who has a different viewpoint than they do. It can teach people to consider the opposite side of the argument and, in some cases, strengthen their beliefs. Some situations cause a change of heart when someone considers the opposing side of the issue, but others serve as proof as to why someone believes what they do. The most important step in learning from other people's perspective is to remember that an opinion is not correct just because someone has always held it. Remaining open to change and changing their mind can be the difference between learning and being obstinate.

When a person is met with an opinion radically different from their own, it can be difficult to remain open-minded and hear the person out if they don't know any techniques with which to regulate themselves. The first step is to refrain from reacting emotionally. Some people are driven by emotion when it comes to hot-button issues, but this is not a good way to establish differences. People should take a moment and think through how they would like to present their opposing opinion before letting their emotions take control. In addition, people should remember it is not helpful to simply shut down when someone expresses a different opinion. If a person is unwilling to even acknowledge someone else's opinion, they will never be able to learn from it and may even create a conflict.

Don't be Afraid to Laugh

Not everyone is confident, and not everyone is sure whether they should point out their flaws or try to make sure no one notices. Despite what most people may think, making certain types of jokes at your own expense can signal confidence and self-assurance. They show that a person is secure enough with their shortcomings to put them on display for others. This confidence shows they can point out a mistake or quirk and laugh along with the group at themselves.

There is a specific way people can actually use self-deprecating humour to build their own self-esteem. It is all about positive self-talk. The key is to phrase the jokes in a particular way so that a person is complimenting themselves and the joke is in their tone of voice. This tactic is effective because people's brains don't necessarily pick up on the tone of how we say things, just the fact that we said them. For example, if Claire says, "I could win the gold medal at running into doors," with a sarcastic tone, her group of friends will probably laugh at the joke. All her brain registered, however, was that she was excelling in an activity.

Self-deprecating humour can be a good way for

someone to relate to others who might be intimidated by their status or title. Making jokes at their own expense can show people that they do not think too highly of themselves and are willing to fit into the group. It can be refreshing for employees to see their boss in casual settings and not be so intimidated by their authority that they are unsure of how to speak to them. Acknowledging flaws can reassure people that someone is still a regular person despite their status or job title. It can show that the power hasn't gone to a person's head. Making jokes at their own expense demonstrates they are not overly concerned with keeping up an authoritative image and persona. This quickly puts other people at ease and encourages normal conversation.

Taking things lightly, seeing the good in people, being open to ideas, and laughing at yourself can all be helpful skills in the dating world too. These tactics can get a person through the first few awkward dates with a new person without it being too painful.

Sometimes going on a blind date can be especially awkward. The two people have never met, are not sure if they have any common interests and have no idea what the other person's emotional or physical boundaries might be. The above-mentioned tactics can help smooth over a rough start by opening an easy conversation and keeping the humour consistent to ease tensions. If someone can also manage to be open minded, then the other person will probably be encouraged to speak more and keep the conversation moving.

Asking open-ended questions can keep the conversation flowing when both people are nervous to speak. It encourages people to build off one another and can be a more natural way to develop conversations. It allows a person to decide how much they want to contribute to a conversation and establish their boundaries if needed. Where yes and no questions can keep a conversation terse and short, open-ended questions are full of possibilities and options for both parties, especially if the subject is something they are mutually interested in. When both parties are interested in the topic, it generates an excitement that can drive conversation for hours. It is a great way to ensure both people have something to contribute. It may take some prodding around to find the right topic to spark excitement, but once it is found, speaking becomes much easier. Using conversational skills on dates demonstrates social aptitude and has the potential to impress others.

9

APPEARANCE MATTERS FOR FIRST IMPRESSIONS

L ooking sharp can be just as important and have an edgy wit when it comes to a successful conversation. When someone is aware of their appearance, they are able to manipulate it in their favour and present a calm, cool and collected persona to others. Part of presenting this image, though, is believing in oneself and having the confidence to dress like an executive or as appropriate for the situation. Clothes play a large role in communicating, and people can use them to show what mood they're in and even what mood they'd like to be in. Along with what someone wears, the way they act in those clothes, or body language, is important as well. People's posture and non-verbal cues can mean more to others than their words, so it is critical that they make sure the messages match. Before initiating a conversation, a person should be sure they are prepared with all the right tools to make sure it is a successful conversation. Tools such as listening, being open and resisting the urge to judge others who are different can all make a huge impact on the success of a conversation or social interaction.

This chapter looks at how appearance is interpreted by others and how a person can manipulate their wardrobe to present the right tone and message. We discuss how people can become more comfortable with their natural appearance and translate that confidence into their wardrobe. We discuss the importance of body language and why people must ensure their non-verbal communication matches their verbal communication.

Appearance Can Be Everything

Appearance, as discussed in Chapter Four, can carry the bulk of the weight in first impressions. People are usually able to determine someone's personality just by observing their appearance — how they dress, their posture, their facial expressions, etc. This is why people should always be aware of how they are presenting them-selves to others and be sure the person they are showing is the person they want others to see. Posture can be a marker of confidence, self-esteem, and respect. Standing straight and letting the shoulder muscles relax goes a long way to show others that someone is comfortable in their own skin. It is a more inviting position than hunching over, which can signal being closed off to others. To match a relaxed posture, a person should make sure their face is relaxed as well. A calm face or smile invites others to approach someone without feeling intimidated and often leads to impromptu interactions. All these factors culminate in an impression, and people can typically gauge someone's level of extroversion, conscientiousness, and openness in this way.

Not all people are confident in their appearance, though, which others may notice unless that person takes steps to start valuing the way they look. The first step is to refuse to conform to mainstream standards. There are a plethora of industries today that thrive on making people think they need certain products to look acceptable. Other industries focus on making people believe they need to be a certain shape to look acceptable. Appearance is a person-by-person standard, though. Someone can find peace with their appearance if they learn to accept who they are and value their differences.

The next step is remembering that it is okay to not look perfect all the time. Working to keep a perfectly primped appearance at all times can be exhausting. People should allow themselves time to be comfortable in their own skin without working to gain approval from others. Smiling can help people feel better about their appearance because it can tell someone's brain to be happy, and it is more difficult to criticise things that make you happy.

The clothes a person chooses to wear shows what mood they're in and can even affect their disposition during the day. When someone gets dressed in the morning, their goal is most likely to be comfortable, which means they will probably pick clothes that match their mood. If someone is feeling nervous, they may choose bigger clothes that they feel hide them from the world. If someone is feeling happy, they might pick bright colours and patterns to stand out in a crowd. This means the way they look will reflect their mood and convey that to others. If someone were to reverse this process, however, they could potentially change their mood based on the clothes they choose to wear.

Dressing to promote the mood a person wants or needs for a specific function is another way to use appearance to their advantage. For a work function, you might want to pick an outfit that makes you feel powerful and confident. A business suit is a classic choice to feel powerful at work. Whether it is a traditional suit, an astounding pantsuit or a simple skirt and blazer, getting dressed up to go to the office can make someone feel more confident and in control than if their wardrobe blends in with those of their coworkers. If someone is going on a first date, they might take a different approach by wearing something that makes them feel comfortable or at ease but is still presentable. The key to dressing for a date is to feel confident and allow your personality to shine through.

Because people are able to evaluate confidence levels based on the way someone is dressed, it is especially important to have some clothes that demonstrate exceptional confidence. Clothes that are tailored to fit just right can make someone feel more attractive and thus more confident. They show others that the person cares enough about making a good impression to make sure their clothes fit perfectly.

Along with appearance, body language shows others how someone is feeling or what they are thinking through non-verbal cues. People read body language much in the same way they interpret appearance, and it can have an impact on their first impressions of a person. Most people trust non-verbal communication (body language) more than verbal communication (speaking). For this reason, it can be helpful for people to be aware of their body language so they are not presenting the wrong message to others. If someone struggles with social anxiety, their default body language may be to close off from others and keep to themselves. Even if that person desires interaction with others, their body language signals that they do not want to be spoken to, so most people may stay away from them. To encourage people to approach them, the person should practice, focusing on keeping an open posture and making eye contact with people as they pass. This allows you to engage others without having to speak and to let them know that, if they would like to talk to you, you are open to a conversation.

Because people typically trust body language over words, if someone is lying or masking the truth, their body language will most likely betray their statements. This can be tricky when someone is conflicted about an issue but does not necessarily want to discuss it with anyone else. If a person asks how they are and they respond with "fine" or "okay" but their body language is visibly distressed, that person will likely insist something is wrong. If someone is troubled about something, but does not want to discuss it, they should focus on changing their verbal messages, not their body language. Because non-verbal communication often happens without people noticing, it can be more difficult to regulate. When someone asks about a sensitive topic, a person could simply respond, "Yes, I'm dealing with a personal issue right now, but I'm not ready to discuss it. Thank you for asking, though." This indicates that the non-verbal cues they noticed are not incorrect but that the topic is not up for discussion.

Playing it Smart

With all the techniques that have been discussed so far, it is clear that conversations take certain mental skills to master. A person can keep their wits sharp and always feel prepared for any interaction if they simply remember the keys to a successful conversation. The first major part of any interaction, as we have already discussed, is listening. If a person is not the speaker, they should focus on understanding the information that is being presented to them so they can then take a moment to process it and answer intelligently. The next step is for a person to be open and express themselves honestly. By presenting a truthful version of themselves, people encourage others to do the same and form a connection. In line with remaining open-minded, people should remember not to judge others for their differences. Not everyone shares the same ideas or opinions, and that's okay. Judging someone for their beliefs is a sure way to end a conversation and should be avoided.

Most conversations meander down a path forged by serendipity. This is because skilled conversationalists often build off of the other person's comments to bring the discussion down new roads and to new topics. It's a simple way to develop an interaction while simultaneously getting to know the other person. Building on topics can sometimes require a little prior knowledge, though, so keeping up with current events and trends can be a wise investment of your time. Some people store away fun facts or interesting articles to discuss with others when a conversation seems to be stalling. In the event the conversation does start to turn bad, a person should have a plan for how to reignite the excitement in the interaction. Offering a change of venue or introducing a completely new discussion are two ways someone can regain control of a stalled conversation. Sometimes, though, it is just time for silence. Being able to embrace silence in a conversation can feel awkward at first, but it is a good way to demonstrate comfort around the other person.

There are a variety of reasons that can lead to silence in a conversation, and someone asking a question the other person does not want to answer is one of them. If someone finds themselves in this situation, there are a few things they can do to evade answering. The first thing, which may be the most important, is to make sure they understand the question. They can ask the person to restate or rephrase the question if they think they may have misinterpreted them. If this doesn't help, they can ask questions about the parts of the question they are uncomfortable with to gain some clarity about why the person is asking this.

Once a person is confident they understand the question, they should take some time to think about their answer or whether or not they will give one. Not all questions need to be answered, and typically, if it makes someone uncomfortable, people will understand if they choose not to respond. If someone is only uncomfortable with part of the question, then they can simply choose to focus on the part they are comfortable with. Answering only part of the question might feel awkward for the speaker, but it is usually sufficient for the asker and can show the person is ready to move on from the topic.

Sometimes, the source of discomfort in a conversation can be a conflict or difference between the two parties. This does not always have to be the end of the interaction, though, if a person knows how to handle the situation. Two keys to resolving a conflict in conversation is to stay open-minded and not to worry about what the other person thinks. Sometimes, a person can get so wrapped up in the belief that someone else is angry with them that it drives their reactions, even if this is not necessarily true. Another useful tactic is to focus on listening to the other person and not speaking. When people dominate a conversation, they do not give the other person a chance to defend or explain themselves. When a person does get a chance to speak, they should be direct and not beat around the bush to get to their point. This can help someone understand what they are feeling and minimise the time spent in conflict. Finally, the person should always aim to find a positive resolution or end to the conversation.

With all the skills discussed in this chapter, you have the ability to lead a successful conversation, but you will still need courage to start. If starting a conversation seems too scary or difficult, you can break it down into sections to make it a little easier. Instead of focusing on how to make it through an entire conversation, you can focus on just one section at a time, such as introducing yourself, breaking the ice, or asking questions. It can be easier to face the fear of initiating interaction if you are in an environment that is familiar and safe. Being somewhere you are used to can make you much more comfortable and reduce the anxiety of being in a new place, in addition to speaking with new people.

When you are new to starting conversations, it can be easier to practice with acquaintances first, rather than perfect strangers. Some may find it easier to strike up small talk with their regular barista at the coffee shop than with whoever might be in line behind them that day.

You should keep in mind that starting to practice conversations will probably feel challenging at first, but the feeling of accomplishment will be worth it in the end. Letting anxiety take control of whether or not you interact with others can be a recipe for isolation. Having the courage to take charge of anxiety can be scary, but knowing a few tactics to overcome the initial discomfort can make the process easier for you. It is important to acknowledge that the task will be challenging. Some people may get discouraged because interacting with others is more difficult for them than it is for others, but if they simply accept that conversations will be a challenge, they can be easier to embrace.

10

ENDING THE CONVERSATION

Saving the best for last, a true conversation master needs to be capable of ending a conversation. It may sound easy enough, but ending interactions on a positive note can be tricky. People need to be able to discern the signs that a conversation is winding down. This can often be determined by how long the conversation has lasted as most people have an expectation of how long interactions will last before they engage with another person. Looking at the other person's body language can tip someone off that their partner is ready to part ways. If someone is yawning, touching their face or no longer making eye contact, they are probably ready to cut ties. People need to have an exit strategy prepared for when they pick up on these subtle cues or they are ready to move on. Letting someone know why the conversation needs to end is one way to wrap things up, as long as it is a legitimate reason. When someone is stuck in a never-ending conversation with a talkative person, they can introduce that person to someone new as a way to leave the conversation without offending the person.

The key to ending conversations is to be direct without seeming rude. Sometimes, a conversational partner will not notice the signs that someone is ready to end the discussion, which might prompt the other person to let them know verbally. It is important to never interrupt someone in an attempt to end a conversation, because it can come across as rude. Once a person is able to establish the end of the conversation, they should politely excuse themselves before leaving. This gives them an opportunity to clarify why they must leave and shows a courtesy to the other person.

This chapter examines the non-verbal cues that signal the end of a conversation and how people can be aware of them in their own interactions. It provides a few exit strategies so that a person can be prepared to leave a conversation if they get stuck in a lengthy discussion. Here is a section about how to politely end conversations and different ways to excuse yourself while making a lasting final impression on someone.

Be Aware

Conversations can be a great way to interact with others, but they are one of those things that is usually enjoyed best in small doses — especially if someone has social anxiety. It can be difficult to tell, though, when a conversation is winding down or when another person is ready to call it quits. Although most people won't come right out and say, "Okay, I'm done," there are more subtle clues a person can look out for to determine if their conversation needs to wrap up soon. Most people have a very general expectation of how long a conversation should last based on the environment and topic. For example, most people expect small talk to be brief, with only a few exchanges. In the break room, people typically exchange a "Hello" and "How is your day going?" and then move back to their respective areas. In more intimate settings, such as someone's dinner party, people can expect conversations to last a little longer because they are in a setting conducive to getting to know someone.

Average conversations last only about 30 minutes. Anything over this, and people might start getting restless and looking for ways to exit the conversation. Especially when speaking to someone they don't know well, people can find lengthy conversations awkward and uninteresting after a time. Despite this common timeframe, people are rarely on the same page with one another as far as how long any given conversation should be. In fact, it could be argued that most of a conversation is two people trying to figure out when to end it. So, if a person ever feels self-conscious about not knowing how to far to take an interaction, they can remember the other person likely feels the same way.

Another simple way to notice if someone is ready for the end of a conversation is to look at their body language while they listen. When someone is ready for a conversation to be over, they often start closing off by crossing their arms or angling themselves away from the speaker. They may start to lose focus on the topic and begin looking at their watch or the door frequently. This usually signals the person has another appointment they need to get to, but they do not want to be rude and simply walk away from the other person. Yawning is also another sign that someone is losing interest.; although most people will attempt to hide a yawn, noticing the tired facial expressions that come with it can be a helpful way to see someone is no longer interested in interacting.

A final sign that a person is ready to part ways is when they are no longer contributing to the conversation. They may be answering in short sentences or with one-word responses. This shows they do not wish to elaborate on the topic further, and it is a good time for the speaker to allow them to exit.

When a person realises it might be time to end a

conversation, there are a few different tactics they can employ to do so gracefully. The important thing to remember is to always be respectful of the speaker and be as polite as possible. No one likes to be cut off or abruptly abandoned when expressing their ideas, so being courteous when ending a conversation can go a long way to showing the other person that, even though someone has to leave, they still value their time and opinions. When a person is ready to make their exit, they should always give a legitimate reason as to why they need to leave the conversation. This shows the other person that having to abandon them is regretful but necessary. The reason should always be legitimate because, if one is made up, the odds are that the other person will see through the lie and take offence to someone lying to end a conversation with them.

A second way to exit a conversation is to use the surroundings as a sort of a buffer. For example, if someone is at a party, they can tell the other person that they would like to go say hello to the host or circulate for a while to meet new people. They can even offer to come back and finish the conversation later in the evening. This is a respectful way to gracefully pull away from someone without making them feel like someone is bailing on the interaction. Using the surroundings can mean using people who are nearby. This tactic works at parties because they are great places to meet new people and make introductions. If a person is stuck in a conversation they are ready to leave, they can introduce the speaker to someone else and pass off the conversation to that person. This way, the person who wants to get away is able to leave, and the person who wants to continue talking still has an audience to interact with.

A person can assume a preemptive approach and lay the groundwork for having to leave before it is time to go. Letting someone know that a person will have to leave at a certain time or within a certain timeframe gives them the opportunity to prepare themselves for an exit, however abrupt it might be. It makes them aware of a time limit, which may result in them helping the person be aware of their self-inflicted restraints and end the conversation on their own.

All these tactics can be difficult to implement, however, if a person is too concerned about following social protocol. Some situations may seem as if there is no polite way out, but with the techniques mentioned above, it can still be simple to exit the conversation. The important thing to remember is that if one person wants out, it's likely the other person does too. So, people should not feel guilty for wanting to leave a conversation early, even if they started it, because all things must come to an end, whether everyone agrees or not.

There are always outliers to these equations, though. Luckily, there are ways to handle them. Some people love to talk with others and might not notice non-verbal cues that their conversation partner wants to end the conversation. This is not uncommon with people who are discussing something they have a deep interest in or passion for or someone who might have a social communication disorder and has trouble interpreting body language and other cues. Just like with other people, it is important to always be respectful and polite in these situations and leave the conversation tactfully so as to leave a positive impression on the other person. People may all interact differently, but at their core, they all have the same basic social needs, and those should always be treated respectfully.

The first step in handling people who are not responding to non-verbal cues is to ensure a person's words match their body language. Similar to what was discussed earlier in this book, people can sometimes become confused when a person's verbal message does not match their body language or other non-verbal communication. If a person seems to not be noticing closed off body language or a lack of eye contact, then a person needs to move to polite but direct verbal messages. Implying that you'd like to further your knowledge of the subject on you own, such as saying "That's a great point. I'd love to research it some," can signal that you are ready to part ways. Someone could even encourage the other person to send them more information, making it clear they'd prefer to continue the conversation via a different medium.

Interrupting someone to end an interaction is never an advisable way to leave a conversation. All people want to be heard, and if someone has been listening to them for a while already, it can particularly disrespectful to interrupt someone and then leave. Silence is a much better tool with which to show others you are no longer willing to participate in the conversation. A person could wait silently while another person finishes their expressing their idea. Often times, the speaker will notice the listener has stopped providing feedback and take this as a sign that they are ready to stop the conversation. Silence can be a much more productive and respectful way to signal the end of an interaction.

If someone feels particularly inclined to interrupt a person, then they should consider interrupting themselves as a way to end the conversation. It might seem unorthodox, but interrupting yourself is a great way to quickly exit a conversation without hurting the other person's feelings. In the middle of a comment, they can simply look at their watch or at a clock, and then say that they just realised the time and will be late for another commitment. This way, the urgency of leaving is established and legitimate, and the person does not have to feel rude about interrupting someone else's speaking time.

Making Your Exit

After explaining why you need to leave a conversation, you still have one more step before you can actually exit. You need to make sure the last thing you do is politely excuse yourself from the person or situation to make a lasting positive impression. It can be easy to give a reason and then leave the room, but taking the time to excuse yourself shows respect and courtesy beyond what might be expected.

The first step in this process is to restate the reason for leaving. This reinforces that leaving is not necessarily by choice but because a person has prior engagements or tasks. You can end by inviting the person to continue the conversation at a later date or through another medium to show you are still interested in the topic at hand.

Another way to make a graceful exit is to summarise the main points of the conversation before leaving the room. This reinforces that you were paying attention to the speaker for the duration of the conversation and valued the information enough to commit it to memory. Being able to summarise the interaction shows you are able to quickly process information and think on your feet.

Finally, you should always thank the other person for the interaction. It may seem superfluous after inviting further conversation or restating why it is important for someone step out, but making a person feel like their time is valued and appreciated can make a memorable impression on them.

At first, excusing yourself may seem awkward. It can be difficult to find the right time and the right words for someone to tactfully excuse themselves from a conversation. The important thing to remember in this situation is that the odds are the other person was ready to end the conversation. Let this thought be a comforting one as the exit is made. You should not feel bad or guilty about leaving a conversation when the time comes. You should not show any discomfort by looking back behind yourself as you leave or asking if it was okay that you exited. Being confident in your exit is just as important as doing it politely.

There are ways to alleviate the awkwardness that might come with making an exit. If the parting happens at work, someone could offer to make plans with the other person to continue the conversation later, maybe at another venue. This establishes that someone doesn't necessarily want to end a discussion but has to leave for other reasons. To do this, sometimes, a person will have to take charge of the situation. Taking control is not a bad thing if the person does it tactfully, as discussed earlier in this chapter. Wait for the other person to finish speaking, then firmly state that there is a reason the conversation needs to end. The key to this is to not leave wiggle room for a person to manipulate the information and thus draw out the conversation even longer.

After leaving a conversation, it is not uncommon for you to begin worrying about whether or not you made a good impression. You may start replaying the conversation in your head to ensure you said all the right things and laughed at all the right jokes. All this anxiety can be avoided, though, if you remember that most people have a positive first impression of who they meet. Most people get so wrapped up in analysing their own behaviour that they don't think about the other person's point of view. They are so busy listening to their inner critic and worrying that their anxiety was visible that they spend more time judging themselves than seeing the conversation for what it was. If they take the time to step back and evaluate the conversation rationally, they will usually see that it went well and the other person was responding positively to them.

People typically create positive first impressions of others after an initial encounter. This is because they typically do not see any anxiety or discomfort a person may be experiencing during the conversation. They are usually focused only on the words and the tone of the conversation, which, if positive, will leave a positive memory and impression. Thus, when someone is scared that they made a bad first impression, they can simply remind themselves that most people like others more than themselves.

To seal the deal with a great impression, you can offer something valuable to the other person just before they leave. This can be a new piece of information, a networking opportunity, an invitation to another event or simply a recognition of their insight. Sometimes, when ending a conversation, you can usually tell your conversation partner is still interested in learning more, so leaving them with a bit of new information to consider can quench their desire to continue discussing the topic at a later date. A networking opportunity can be incredibly exciting for people, especially budding professionals, and are all the more special when they do not need to be requested. Offering an introduction to someone in an industry or office can show that someone believes in the other person and is willing to vouch for the abilities.

11

SUMMARY

Interacting with others can be a daunting task for people with social anxiety. It may seem too difficult or scary a task to even approach at times. Many typical people, however, feel this way too when engaging socially with others. Those with social anxiety may have to put in a little extra effort to start a conversation, but the skills discussed in this book are universal.

Preparation

Before you can feel confident about starting a conversation, you should first attempt to assess your personality style. Understanding your own personality, temperament and social needs can vastly affect the types of conversations you will feel comfortable in and how frequently you engage with others. Part of this understanding is realising the negative effects loneliness can have and making efforts to counteract them. Connecting with others is a powerful tool and can combat loneliness while promoting empathy. Empathy is one of the best tools you can use when attempting to interact with others because it can help you understand and relate to them better.

When deciphering how a conversation might play out, you should always remember that listening plays just as important a role as speaking. Using active listening techniques can demonstrate attentiveness and make the speaker feel valued and appreciated. Looking at people while they speak can also help you retain more information than if you were distracted during a conversation. The final bit of preparation you will need to start a conversation is to know how to inject yourself into an established group. If you can find a way to smoothly integrate into a group conversation, you can feel like a conversational master.

Action

Once you are prepared to start a conversation with someone, it is time for you to focus on their actions. Taking the environment and context of a conversation into account before making any moves is a great way to ensure you are respecting any boundaries or unspoken rules that may precede the interaction. After establishing the type of conversation you are going to engage in, you should continue to treat people courteously and respect any boundaries that are presented. You can laugh and keep conversations light so you and the participants stay open and interested.

After getting the hang of speaking to others, you can begin to acknowledge how their appearance affects your perceptions of them. Appearance does matter, especially when forming a first impression of someone. Dressing for the occasion or to show confidence both take practice, but they are worth the effort in the end. Finally, knowing how to tactfully end a conversation is the piece de resistance of any skilled conversationalist.

After reading this book, I hope you feel confident about the process of facing your fears and having conversations with others.

THANK YOU!

Thank you for buying and reading this book. If you enjoyed what you read, then I would be grateful if you could leave a review on Amazon, Goodreads, or the store that you bought the book from.

ALSO AVAILABLE FROM STEPHEN HAUNTS

https://geni.us/thepathtofreedom

Made in United States
North Haven, CT
23 August 2024